DR. ASH PACHAURI, PhD
&
DR. SAROJ PACHAURI, MD, PhD, DPH

Climate Action Now

A Practical Guide to Building a Sustainable Future One Step at a Time

Contents

Book 1

CLIMATE SERIES

Small Steps, Big Impact
A Simple Guide to Individual Action and Collective Impact to Tackle Climate Change

by
Dr. Ash Pachauri & Dr. Saroj Pachauri

Prelude

D uring the release of the AR5 Synthesis Report in 2014, the then Chief of the Nobel Peace Laureate, Intergovernmental Panel on Climate Change, Dr. Rajendra Pachauri said "nobody on this planet" will be untouched by the impacts of climate change.

He said climate change will reduce water availability, cause species to migrate, harm crop yields, and bring more damaging extreme weather. Human security will likely be shaped by increased displacement and conflict, made worse by climate stresses, and some low-lying states may face a loss of their territory.

Climate change is for real. We have just a small window of opportunity and it is closing rather rapidly. There is not a moment to lose.

Dr. R. K. Pachauri, Former Chairman IPCC (2002-2015)

Small Steps, Big Impact

C limate change, an urgent and existential challenge of our time, is a global phenomenon that spares no one. Its far-reaching consequences threaten our existence, global economy, peace, and societal survival. In this chapter, we will delve into the science of climate change, exploring its causes, effects, and implications.

Understanding the Science of Climate Change

Climate change, which encompasses long-term shifts in temperature, precipitation patterns, and other aspects of the Earth's climatic system, is a complex phenomenon. While natural factors such as volcanic eruptions and variations in solar radiation have influenced climate and weather patterns throughout history, the current nature, pace, and magnitude of climate change, as we know it today, are primarily driven by human activity.

The leading cause of climate change, influenced by human activities, is the release of certain gases into the air. These gases, like carbon dioxide, methane, and nitrous oxide, trap heat from the sun in the Earth's atmosphere, leading to a warming effect known as the greenhouse effect. While some of these gases occur naturally, human activities, such as burning fossil fuels, cutting down forests, and industrial processes, have significantly increased their levels in the atmosphere, especially since the Industrial Revolution.

Consequences of Climate Change

The impacts of climate change are varied and wide-ranging, affecting the Earth's ecosystems, economies, and people worldwide. No corner of the globe is left untouched by climate change's impacts. Some of the most notable consequences include:

1. **Rising temperatures:** Global temperatures have increased over the past century, leading to more frequent, extreme, and intense heat waves. The warming of Earth's temperatures has severe implications for human health, agriculture, water resources, food security, displacement of communities, and human security overall.

2. **Changing weather patterns:** Climate change has altered precipitation patterns, leading to more frequent and extreme weather events, including droughts, floods, and storms. These extreme weather events cause widespread damage to infrastructure, crops and agriculture, and environmental ecosystems.

3. **Warming of ocean temperatures, melting ice caps, and rising sea levels:** The warming climate results in sea-level rise. This poses a significant threat to coastal ecosystems and communities due to increasing the risk of flooding and erosion.

4. **Loss of biodiversity:** In the relentless pursuit of 'progress' through industrialization and urbanization, humans have destroyed natural plant and animal habitats through deforestation. Natural ecosystem and habitat loss have, in turn, led to shifts in and loss of flora and fauna, resulting in the permanent extinction of several species. Such biodiversity loss has cascading effects on natural ecosystem balances such as pollination, pest control, disease mitigation, and water purification.

Implications for Society

The impacts of climate change are not evenly distributed, with the most vulnerable and marginalized communities often bearing the greatest brunt of the consequences. Vulnerable populations, including low-income groups, indigenous communities, and people living in coastal or arid regions, are the most impacted and disproportionately affected by climate-related disasters and disruptions.

Furthermore, climate change exacerbates existing social and economic inequalities, creating new challenges for sustainable development and poverty alleviation efforts. Addressing climate change requires not only eliminating carbon from the atmosphere and reducing greenhouse gas emissions to mitigate the impacts of climate change but also building resilience and adaptive capacity within communities to cope with its impacts.

Conclusion

In conclusion, climate change is a complex and multifaceted issue with far-reaching implications for the planet and all its inhabitants. Understanding the science behind climate change is essential for taking knowledge-inspired initiatives to develop effective strategies to mitigate its impacts and adapt to a changing climate. In the following chapters, we will explore the role that individuals can play by taking concrete action in their daily lives, not just to tackle the challenge of climate change but also to build a more sustainable future for future generations.

At this juncture, it's crucial to recognize that while climate change undeniably presents an existential threat to all life forms and the very existence of our planet, there exists a narrow window of opportunity for us to act and address its impacts. Nevertheless, it's imperative to acknowledge that swift action is essential, as this window is rapidly closing. Despite this urgency, as individuals, we possess the power to instigate the necessary change. By educating ourselves about our role in combatting climate change and committing to action promptly, we can seize this opportunity for transformation. History has shown that pivotal moments that reshaped the course of humanity arose from the collective efforts of individuals and society. Just as Mahatma Gandhi advocated, we have the capacity to "be the change we want to see in the world." We have done it before, and we can do it again. Considering our lives and livelihoods hinge upon it, what more significant existential challenge could unite humanity and spur us to effect change?

The Power of Individual Action

In the face of daunting global challenges like climate change, it's easy to feel powerless as individuals. However, history has repeatedly demonstrated that individual actions can lead to significant change when magnified and multiplied. In this chapter, we will explore the power of individual action in tackling climate change and building a more sustainable future for our planet and future generations.

The Significance of Individual Actions

While the scale of climate change may seem overwhelming, it is essential to recognize that every action we take as individuals has an impact, no matter how small. Whether it's reducing our carbon footprint by reducing our energy usage, reducing our consumption and altering our buying habits, minimizing waste, or advocating for policy change, each individual has the power to contribute to the collective effort to tackle climate change.

Moreover, individual actions can be powerful examples and catalysts for more significant and broader change. When magnified, others see their friends, family, and neighbors taking steps to reduce their carbon footprint; they are more likely to follow suit, creating a ripple effect that can lead to the widespread adoption of sustainable practices.

Case Studies of Individual Impact

Throughout history, individuals from all walks of life have played critical roles in driving progress on environmental goals. From grassroots activists organizing community clean-up events to scientists and inventors developing innovative technologies to combat climate change, individual actions have been instrumental in advancing progress on the sustainability agenda.

Take, for instance, the POP Movement, an acronym for Protect Our Planet, a global climate initiative primarily driven by youth (learn more at www.thepopmovement.org), which was co-founded by the late Dr. R.K. Pachauri (visit www.rkpachauri.org), former Chairman of the Intergovernmental Panel on Climate Change (2002-2015) who, alongside former Vice President Al Gore, was awarded the Nobel Peace Prize in 2007. This movement, described in more detail in subsequent books in this series, underscores the imperative for individual and collective efforts, innovation, and a steadfast commitment to environmental stewardship. Across 129 countries, the POP Movement has inspired over two million young individuals and fostered 431 partnerships, mobilizing masses to take tangible climate action. Youth activists within the POP Movement are at the forefront, spearheading numerous climate projects, capacity-building endeavors, and educational campaigns worldwide (please visit https://thepo pmovement.org/projects/ for more information). However, these endeavors represent only a fraction of the comprehensive response required to mitigate our planet's peril. As aptly expressed by the late Dr. R.K. Pachauri, "Nobody on this planet is going to be untouched by the impacts of climate change." Hence, the POP Movement urgently beckons all global citizens to rally together, leveraging the power of community, knowledge, and diversity to safeguard our planet for future generations.

Overcoming Psychological Barriers

While the potential for individual action to make a significant difference, as witnessed by the POP Movement and other initiatives, is vast and critical, many people confront psychological barriers preventing them from addressing climate change. These barriers may include feelings of helplessness, anxiety, denial, or apathy, as well as concerns about the perceived inconvenience or cost of adopting sustainable behaviors.

Overcoming these barriers requires a shift in mindset, changes in lifestyle and behavior, and a recognition of the interconnectedness of individual actions and their collective impact. By reframing climate change as an opportunity for positive change rather than an insurmountable challenge, individuals can empower themselves to take meaningful action and inspire others to do the same.

Conclusion

In conclusion, the power of individual action must be balanced when addressing climate change. By recognizing our capacity to make a difference and taking proactive steps to reduce our environmental impact, each of us has the potential to contribute to building a sustainable future. In the following chapters, we will explore practical strategies for individuals to take action on climate change in their everyday lives.

Reducing Carbon Footprint

One highly impactful approach to addressing climate change involves individuals lowering their carbon footprint. A carbon footprint represents the collective greenhouse gas emissions directly or indirectly generated by a person, entity, product, or occasion. This chapter will delve into practical methods for individuals to shrink their carbon footprint, thereby reducing their emissions and resulting environmental impact.

Practical Strategies for Energy Efficiency

1. Home Energy Conservation

Improve insulation: Proper building and home insulation can significantly reduce carbon emissions and heating and cooling costs by minimizing heat loss in the winter and heat gain in the summer.

Upgrade to energy-efficient appliances: Replace old, inefficient appliances with ENERGY STAR-certified appliances that use less energy and reduce greenhouse gas emissions.

Use programmable thermostats: Programmable thermostats allow individuals to automatically adjust temperature settings, saving energy when they are away or asleep.

Switch off lights: Switching off lights when unnecessary is a simple yet effective way to reduce energy consumption.

Here are some tips to make it easier:

a. Install Sensors: Consider installing motion or occupancy sensors in rooms where lights are frequently left on. These sensors can automatically turn off lights when no one is in the room.

b. Use Timers: Set timers for lights in areas where lights may be left on when not in use, such as outdoor lights or lights in common areas.

c. Natural Light: Make the most of natural light during the day by keeping curtains and blinds open. This can reduce the need for artificial lighting. Also, (re)arranging living space and furniture to make the most of natural light during the day can reduce the need for artificial lighting.

d. Switch to LED Bulbs: LED bulbs consume significantly less energy than traditional incandescent bulbs. They also last longer, saving money in the long run.

e. Educate Household Members: Encourage everyone in your household to be mindful of turning off lights when leaving a room. Developing the habit may take some time, but it can greatly affect energy savings.

f. Designated Switches: Designate specific switches for groups of lights to make it easier to turn off multiple lights at once when leaving a room.

g. Regular Maintenance: Ensure that light fixtures and bulbs are well-maintained. Clean fixtures and dust-free bulbs can distribute light more effectively, reducing the need for additional lighting.

h. Disconnect Unused Devices: Disconnect or unplug devices and gadgets not currently in use to minimize unnecessary power consumption and energy usage.

By implementing these simple practices, individuals can contribute to reducing energy consumption and lowering electricity bills.

2. Renewable Energy Sources

Install solar panels: Generating electricity from solar panels reduces reliance on fossil fuels and lowers greenhouse gas emissions associated with electricity production.

Green design and architecture: Green homes and buildings are designed and constructed with sustainability in mind, and one aspect of that is often integrating renewable energy sources into design and infrastructure.

Here's how green buildings can tap into renewable energy:

a. Solar Power: As mentioned above, installing solar panels on rooftops or building facades is one of the most common ways for green buildings to tap into renewable energy. Solar photovoltaic (PV) systems convert sunlight into electricity, providing a clean and sustainable power source.

b. Wind Power: In some locations, wind turbines can be integrated into the design of green buildings to harness wind energy. However, this is more common in more significant commercial or industrial buildings with ample space for turbine installation.

c. Geothermal Energy: Green buildings can utilize geothermal heat pumps to tap into the Earth's stable underground temperatures for heating and cooling. Geothermal systems are highly efficient and can significantly reduce a home or building's energy consumption and carbon footprint.

d. Biomass Energy: Biomass energy, derived from organic materials such as wood, agricultural residues, or organic waste, can be used for heating or electricity generation in green buildings. Biomass boilers or biogas digesters can be installed to harness this renewable energy source.

e. Hydropower: While less common for individual buildings, hydropower can be utilized in specific locations with access to flowing water. Micro-hydro systems can generate electricity for on-site use or feed excess power back into the grid.

f. Combined Heat and Power (CHP): Also known as cogeneration, CHP systems simultaneously generate electricity and proper heat from a single fuel source, such as natural gas or biomass. Green buildings can incorporate CHP systems to maximize energy efficiency and reduce reliance on grid-supplied electricity.

g. Passive Design Strategies: Besides active renewable energy systems, green buildings often employ passive design strategies to optimize energy efficiency. These may include orientation to maximize natural light and ventilation, high-performance insulation, and thermal mass to regulate indoor temperatures.

By tapping into renewable energy sources, green buildings reduce their environmental impact and often achieve long-term cost savings through reduced energy costs and increased resilience to energy price fluctuations.

3. Transportation Options

Choose sustainable modes of transportation: To reduce reliance on fossil fuel-powered vehicles, walk, bike, carpool, or use public transit whenever possible.

Drive fuel-efficient vehicles: When purchasing a new car, choose a fuel-efficient option with low emissions or consider transitioning to an electric or hybrid vehicle.

4. Refuse, Reduce, Reuse, Recycle

While reducing, reusing, and recycling is effective in reducing an individual's environmental footprint, considering the challenges associated with recycling, particularly in the case of plastic, it's advisable to give precedence to refusing, reducing, and reusing. For example, opting out of single-use plastic straws is a straightforward individual action.

Minimize waste generation: Reduce consumption of single-use products and opt for reusable alternatives whenever possible.

Recycle responsibly: Properly recycle paper, glass, plastic, and metal materials to conserve resources and reduce greenhouse gas emissions associated with landfilling and incineration.

Proper waste management is crucial in promoting sustainability in several ways, as described below:

a. Resource Conservation: Effective waste management facilitates the recovery and recycling of resources, such as metals, paper, and plastic.

b. Reduced Environmental Impact: Proper waste management minimizes pollution and environmental degradation by controlling the release of harmful substances into the air, water, and soil. This helps protect ecosystems and preserve biodiversity.

c. Energy Recovery: Some waste management practices, such as waste-to-energy facilities and anaerobic digestion, can convert organic waste into renewable energy sources, contributing to the transition to a low-carbon economy and reducing reliance on fossil fuels.

d. Mitigating Climate Change: Waste management can significantly reduce greenhouse gas emissions by diverting organic waste from landfills and utilizing methane capture technologies, thus mitigating climate change impacts.

e. Promoting a Circular Economy: Waste management systems that prioritize recycling, composting, and product reuse contribute to the principles of a circular economy by keeping materials in use for as long as possible, minimizing waste generation, and fostering resource efficiency.

f. Contributing to Community Health and Well-being: Proper waste management practices improve public health by reducing exposure to hazardous materials and preventing the spread of diseases associated with improperly disposed waste.

Effective waste management strategies are essential for achieving sustainability goals by conserving resources, protecting the environment, mitigating climate change, and enhancing community well-being.

5. Dietary Choices and Carbon Emissions

Reduce meat consumption: Livestock farming, particularly beef and lamb, is a significant source of methane emissions and requires large amounts of land and water resources. Choosing a plant-based or vegetarian diet or reducing meat consumption can significantly reduce an individual's carbon footprint.

Choose sustainably sourced seafood: Overfishing and unsustainable fishing practices contribute to habitat destruction and biodiversity loss. Choose sustainably sourced seafood options certified by organizations such as the Marine Stewardship Council (MSC) or Seafood Watch.

Support local and organic agriculture: Choosing locally grown and organic produce reduces the carbon emissions associated with transportation, refrigeration, synthetic fertilizers, and pesticides.

Minimize food waste: Approximately one-third of all food produced globally is wasted, contributing to greenhouse gas emissions from land-fills. Minimize food waste by planning meals, storing food properly, and composting organic waste.

By implementing these strategies, individuals can significantly reduce their carbon footprint and contribute to the collective effort to combat climate change. Additionally, reducing energy consumption and transitioning to renewable energy sources can lead to cost savings, improve air quality, and create a more sustainable future for future generations.

Conclusion

In conclusion, reducing the individual carbon footprint is essential for mitigating the impacts of climate change and transitioning to a more sustain-able society. Individuals can play a vital role in addressing climate change by adopting energy-efficient practices, transitioning to renewable energy sources, making conscious choices about transportation and consumption habits, and altering diets. In the following chapters, we will explore ways individuals can take action to promote sustainability and environmental preservation.

Sustainable Consumption

Consumer choices significantly impact the environment, from the products that individuals buy to how waste is managed and disposed. Sustainable consumption involves making choices that minimize environmental impact, conserve resources, and promote social equity. This chapter will explore how individuals can adopt sustainable consumption behaviors to reduce their ecological footprint and contribute to a more sustainable planet.

Understanding Environmental Impact

Before making purchasing and consumption decisions, it's essential to understand the environmental impact of individual product and service choices. This includes considering resource extraction, manufacturing processes, transportation, the use phase, and end-of-life product disposal. Individuals can minimize their contribution to pollution, resource depletion, and habitat destruction by choosing products with lower environmental footprints.

Principles of Sustainable Consumption

1. Reduce Consumption

Practice minimalism: Simplify your lifestyle by decluttering and focusing on experiences rather than material possessions.

Avoid impulse buying: Consider whether it is necessary and aligns with your values and sustainability goals before purchasing.

2. Choose Sustainable Products

Look for eco-labels and certifications: Choose products certified by reputable organizations such as Fair Trade. Choose locally sourced organic products to ensure that they meet environmental and social standards.

Consider the product's lifecycle: Choose durable, repairable, and recyclable products to minimize waste and resource consumption.

3. Support Sustainable Brands

Research companies' sustainability practices. Support brands that prioritize environmental stewardship, ethical labor practices, and transparency in their supply chains.

Consider the social impact: Choose products from companies that support fair wages, worker rights, and community development initiatives.

4. Reduce Waste

Practice the 4Rs: Refuse, reduce, reuse, recycle. Minimize waste generation by refusing products and choosing products with minimal packaging, reusing items whenever possible, and recycling materials that cannot be avoided.

Compost organic waste: Composting food scraps and yard waste reduces methane emissions from landfills and produces nutrient-rich soil for gardening.

5. Promote Circular Economy

Choose products with circular design principles: Support products and businesses that embrace circular economy principles, such as designing products for durability, repairability, and recyclability.

Participate in sharing and rental platforms: Reduce resource consumption by sharing or renting items such as tools, clothes, and electronics instead of purchasing new ones.

By adopting principles of sustainable consumption, individuals can reduce their ecological footprint, conserve natural resources, and promote a more equitable and sustainable economy. Through informed choices and responsible consumption habits, individuals can contribute to a brighter future for both people and the planet.

Conclusion

In conclusion, sustainable consumption is essential for addressing environmental challenges such as climate change, resource depletion, and pollution. By adopting the principles of refuse, reduce, reuse, and recycle and supporting sustainable brands and products, individuals can minimize their environmental impact and contribute to the transition to a more sustainable society. In the following chapters, we will explore ways individuals can take action to promote sustainability in their daily lives and communities.

Advocacy and Community Engagement

W hile individual actions are essential, collective efforts are needed to address systemic issues such as climate change. Advocacy and community engagement are crucial in driving policy change, mobilizing resources, and fostering collaboration to address environmental challenges. In this chapter, we will explore strategies for individuals to become advocates for climate action and engage with their communities to promote sustainability.

Understanding Advocacy

Advocacy involves speaking up for a cause, raising awareness about issues, and influencing policy decision-makers to take action. Climate advocacy encompasses various activities, from grassroots organizing and community outreach to lobbying policymakers and participating in public discourse. By engaging in advocacy, individuals can magnify community action and amplify their voices about affecting change at local, national, and global levels.

Strategies for Climate Advocacy

1. Educate Yourself

Stay informed about climate science, policy developments, and advocacy opportunities through reputable and credible sources such as scientific journals, accurate news outlets, and environmental organizations.

Educate others through conversations, publications, presentations, and social media about the impacts of climate change and the urgency of taking action.

2. Engage with Policymakers

Contact elected officials: Write letters, emails, or phone your representatives urging them to support policies that address climate change, such as renewable energy incentives, carbon pricing, and emissions reduction targets.

Attend town hall meetings and public hearings: Participate in public forums to voice your concerns about climate change and advocate for policy solutions.

3. Mobilize Your Community

Organize events and workshops: Host educational events, film screenings, dialogue, and workshops to raise awareness about climate change and empower others to take action.

Build coalitions: Collaborate with local organizations, businesses, and community groups to coordinate collective action on climate issues and amplify your impact. Demand urgent action from elected officials and only elect representatives who support climate-friendly policies.

4. Support Climate Justice

Center equity and justice: Advocate for climate policies that prioritize the needs of marginalized communities and address the disproportionate impacts of climate change on the most vulnerable populations that have contributed the least to the issue of climate change.

Amplify diverse voices: Elevate the voices of communities and indigenous peoples directly impacted by climate change and at the frontline of environmental injustice.

5. Use Individual Influence

Use Individual platform/s: As an influencer, business leader, investor, consumer, or community organizer, leverage individual influence to raise awareness about climate change and promote sustainable practices. Promote demand for sustainable products, services, and supply chains. Support green and clean businesses. Vote into power the officials who support sustainable practices and environmental action.

Support divestment: Advocate for divestment from fossil fuels and investment in renewable energy and sustainable initiatives within your workplace, community, home, or school.

Individuals can drive meaningful change and contribute to collective efforts to address climate change and promote sustainability by engaging in advocacy and community engagement. Individuals can build a more resilient and equitable future for all through collaboration, education, and action.

Conclusion

In conclusion, advocacy and community engagement are essential for addressing climate change and fostering sustainable development. Advocating for policy change, mobilizing resources, and empowering communities can be crucial in driving systemic change and building a more sustainable future. In the following chapters, we will explore ways individuals can take action to promote environmental stewardship and create positive change in their communities.

Investing in the Future

I nvesting in sustainability is not just about protecting the environment; it's also about securing a more prosperous and equitable future for future generations. This chapter will explore how individuals can align their financial decisions with their values by investing in companies and initiatives that promote environmental action, social responsibility, and long-term sustainability.

Understanding Sustainable Investment

Sustainable investment, also known as socially responsible investing or Environmental, Social, and Governance (ESG) investing, involves considering environmental, social, and governance factors alongside financial returns when making investment decisions. By investing in companies with strong ESG practices, individuals can support businesses prioritizing sustainability and responsible business practices.

Strategies for Sustainable Investing

1. Research Sustainable Investment Options

Explore ESG funds: Invest in mutual funds, exchange-traded funds (ETFs), or index funds that integrate ESG criteria into their investment strategies.

Consider impact investing: Direct your investments towards projects and companies that generate positive social and environmental outcomes, such as renewable energy, clean technology, or sustainable agriculture.

2. Divest from Fossil Fuels

Avoid investments in fossil fuel companies: Divest from companies involved in the extraction, production, or distribution of fossil fuels, such as coal, oil, and natural gas.

Support renewable energy: Invest in companies that develop and deploy renewable energy technologies, such as solar, wind, and hydropower.

3. Engage with Companies

Vote your shares: Exercise your shareholder voting rights to support resolutions that promote sustainability, transparency, and accountability within companies.

Engage in shareholder activism: Advocate for corporate policies and practices that align with sustainability goals by engaging with company management and participating in shareholder meetings.

4. Consider Long-Term Value

Assess risks and opportunities: Evaluate companies based on their long-term sustainability performance, including environmental action, social impact, and governance practices.

Look beyond immediate financial returns: Consider your investments' broader societal and environmental impacts and potential to generate positive change over the long term.

5. Support Sustainable Finance Initiatives

Invest in green bonds: Purchase bonds to finance environmental projects, such as renewable energy infrastructure, energy efficiency retrofits, or sustainable transportation initiatives.

Explore community investing: Support community development initiatives, affordable housing projects, and small businesses through community development financial institutions or impact investing platforms.

By incorporating sustainability into investment decisions, individuals can achieve financial goals and contribute to positive social and environmental outcomes. Through conscious investing, individuals have the power to drive capital toward businesses and initiatives that prioritize sustainability and create value for society.

Conclusion

In conclusion, investing in sustainability is a powerful way for individuals to align their financial resources with their values and contribute to positive social and environmental change. By integrating environmental, social, and governance factors into investment decisions, individuals can support businesses that prioritize sustainability and drive positive change. In the following chapters, we will explore ways individuals can take action to promote sustainability and create a more resilient future for all.

Education and Awareness

E ducation and awareness are crucial in promoting climate action and supporting sustainability. By increasing environmental literacy, raising awareness about the impacts of human activities on the planet, and empowering individuals to take knowledge-inspired climate action, we can create a more informed, inspired, and engaged society. In this chapter, we will explore the importance of education and awareness in the context of climate action and provide strategies for promoting environmental literacy in schools, workplaces, and communities.

The Importance of Environmental Education

Environmental education provides individuals with the knowledge, skills, and attitudes to understand and address complex environmental issues such as climate change. By integrating ecological topics into formal education curricula and informal learning experiences, we can equip future generations with the tools they need to become responsible citizens of the planet who exercise sustainable practices irrespective of their field of specialization or work.

Strategies for Promoting Environmental Education

1. Integrate Environmental Topics into Education Curricula

Incorporate the science of climate change and sustainability activities into school curricula at all levels, from elementary to higher education, across various subjects, including science, social studies, and civics.

Provide hands-on learning experiences such as outdoor education, field trips, and environmental projects to engage students in real-world environmental issues and solutions.

2. Teacher Training and Professional Development

Offer training and resources for educators to enhance their knowledge and teaching skills in environmental education and sustainability.

Provide opportunities for educators to collaborate, share best practices, and develop interdisciplinary curriculum materials that integrate environmental topics into existing lesson plans.

3. Promote Environmental Literacy in the Workplace

Offer environmental awareness training and sustainability workshops to employees to increase their awareness of their work's environmental impact and promote sustainable workplace practices.

Encourage employee engagement in sustainability initiatives such as energy conservation, consumption habits, waste reduction, and green commuting options.

4. Community Outreach and Engagement

Partner with local organizations, non-profits, and government agencies to host community events, workshops, and educational programs on environmental topics such as climate change, recycling, and sustainable living. Help communities understand the implications of unsustainable consumption and production on human health, economy, and security.

Foster collaboration and networking among community members, businesses, and government stakeholders to develop collective solutions to environmental challenges.

5. Use Digital and Media Platforms

Utilize digital platforms, social media, media, and multimedia resources to disseminate information, raise awareness, advocate, and engage audiences in environmental issues and solutions.

Create educational content such as videos, podcasts, infographics, and online courses to reach diverse audiences and inspire climate action and sustainability.

By promoting environmental education and awareness, we can empower individuals to make informed decisions, adopt sustainable behaviors, consume sustainably, and become agents of positive change in their communities and beyond. Through collaborative efforts across sectors, we can build a more environmentally literate and resilient society capable of addressing the challenges of climate change and creating a sustainable future for all.

Conclusion

In conclusion, education and awareness are essential pillars of effective climate action and environmental sustainability. By prioritizing ecological education in schools, workplaces, and communities, we can cultivate a culture of change and empower individuals to impact the planet positively. In the chapters that follow, we will explore additional ways individuals and communities can take action to promote environmental literacy and create a sustainable future.

Building Resilience

A s the impacts of climate change become increasingly evident, building resilience has become a critical priority for communities worldwide. Resilience involves the ability to anticipate, prepare for, and adapt to the challenges posed by a changing climate while minimizing vulnerability and promoting sustainability. In this chapter, we will explore strategies for building resilience at the individual, community, and societal levels to mitigate the impacts of climate change and foster adaptation.

Understanding Climate Resilience

Climate resilience encompasses a range of strategies and approaches to reduce communities' and ecosystems' vulnerability to climate-related hazards such as extreme weather events, sea-level rise, and shifting precipitation patterns. By building resilience, communities can better withstand and recover from the impacts of climate change while also promoting long-term sustainability and well-being.

Strategies for Building Resilience

1. Risk Assessment and Planning

Conduct vulnerability assessments: Identify areas and populations most at risk of climate change impacts, such as coastal communities, low-lying areas, and regions prone to droughts or wildfires.

Develop climate adaptation plans: Collaborate with communities and stakeholders to develop comprehensive adaptation plans that prioritize actions to reduce vulnerability, enhance resilience, and promote sustainable development.

2. Infrastructure and Design

Invest in resilient infrastructure: Upgrade and retrofit critical infrastructure such as transportation networks, water and wastewater systems, and energy grids to withstand climate-related hazards, including extreme heatwaves, wildfires, and flooding.

Incorporate green infrastructure: Integrate nature-based solutions such as green roofs, permeable pavement, and restored wetlands to manage stormwater, reduce flooding, and enhance biodiversity.

3. Community Engagement and Empowerment

Foster community resilience: Engage with community members to identify local priorities, strengths, and vulnerabilities, and empower them to participate in resilience-building efforts and take ownership of their actions by leading them.

Support social cohesion: Strengthen social networks, community connections, and mutual aid networks to enhance resilience and promote collective action in response to climate impacts.

Involve local communities in crafting and executing solutions at the grassroots level, ensuring that initiatives are tailored to and embraced by the communities they serve. This approach empowers communities to take ownership of local solutions, thus building their capacity for sustained action. As the adage goes, "Give a man a fish, and you feed him for a day. Teach a man to fish, and you feed him for a lifetime."

4. Ecosystem Restoration and Conservation

Protect and restore natural ecosystems: Preserve and restore forests, wetlands, and coastal habitats to enhance their resilience to climate change, sequester carbon, and provide ecosystem services such as flood protection and water purification.

Promote biodiversity conservation: Protect biodiversity hotspots and endangered species to maintain ecosystem resilience and adaptability in the face of climate change.

5. Adaptive Governance and Policy

Implement adaptive governance structures: Establish flexible and inclusive decision-making processes that respond effectively to changing climate conditions, community voices, and evolving community needs.

Integrate climate resilience into policy and planning: To minimize the risk of climate disasters and promote sustainability, incorporate climate resilience considerations into land use planning, zoning regulations, building codes, and infrastructure investments.

By implementing these strategies, communities can enhance their resilience to climate change, reduce vulnerability, and promote long-term sustainability and well-being. Building resilience requires collaboration, innovation, and a commitment to addressing the root causes of vulnerability while adapting to the challenges posed by a changing climate over time.

Conclusion

In conclusion, building resilience is essential for addressing the impacts of climate change and promoting sustainable development. By investing in risk assessment, infrastructure upgrades, community engagement, ecosystem conservation, and adaptive governance, communities can enhance their capacity to withstand and recover from climate-related hazards. The following chapter will explore ways individuals' actions can impact global communities.

The Power of Collective Action

I t's evident now that individual actions are feasible and crucial in addressing the urgent issue of climate change. Furthermore, the cumulative effect of each action, along with its potential to inspire change, holds the promise of propelling a widespread movement of collective action. This collective effort is essential for confronting the systemic challenges of climate change. The power of collective action lies in the ability of individuals, communities, organizations, and governments to come together to tackle shared problems and create positive change. This chapter will explore the importance of cumulative and collective action in addressing climate change, highlight successful initiatives and movements, and discuss how individual actions can contribute to collective efforts for a more sustainable future.

The Interconnectedness of Collective Action

Climate change is a global challenge that requires coordinated action at all levels of society. By working together, individuals, communities, businesses, and governments can leverage their resources, expertise, and influence to implement more effective, equitable, and sustainable solutions than individual efforts alone. Collective action also fosters solidarity, builds social capital, and creates momentum for change by demonstrating the power of collaboration and cooperation.

Examples of Collective Action

1. Global Climate Movements

Guided by young leaders, the POP Movement has rallied millions worldwide to combat climate change. Through the coordination of educational events, advocacy initiatives, and the implementation of technological solutions, youth within the POP Movement are confronting the climate crisis by focusing on local solutions tailored to and led by communities themselves. Moreover, they actively advocate with global governments and corporations to enact substantive policy changes.

2. Community Renewable Energy Projects

Community-led renewable energy projects, such as solar cooperatives and wind farms, have empowered local communities to take control of their energy future and transition to clean, renewable power sources. By pooling resources and expertise, communities can reduce energy costs, create local jobs, and reduce greenhouse gas emissions.

3. Divestment Campaigns

Divestment campaigns have urged institutions such as universities, pension funds, and religious organizations to divest from fossil fuel investments and reinvest in clean energy and sustainable initiatives. By targeting the financial industry, divestment campaigns have helped shift capital away from fossil fuels and towards renewable energy while raising awareness about the economic risks of investing in fossil fuels.

4. International Agreements and Treaties

International agreements such as the Paris Agreement provide frameworks for countries to collaborate to mitigate greenhouse gas emissions, adapt to climate change's impacts, and support developing countries in their efforts to transition to low-carbon economies. International agreements play a crucial role in addressing climate change globally by fostering cooperation and collaboration among nations.

Contributing to Collective Action

While collective action often requires coordination and collaboration among diverse stakeholders, individuals can also be crucial in driving change through their actions, advocacy, and engagement. By participating in community initiatives, supporting grassroots movements, voting for climate-conscious leaders, and advocating for policy change, individuals can contribute to collective efforts to address climate change and create a more sustainable future for all.

Conclusion

In conclusion, the power of collective action is essential for addressing the complex and interconnected challenges posed by climate change. By working together, individuals, communities, organizations, and governments can harness their collective resources, expertise, and influence to implement more effective, equitable, and sustainable solutions than individual efforts alone. In the following section, we will explore additional ways individuals can contribute to collective action and create positive change in their communities and worldwide.

Embracing the Challenge

The Way Forward

Addressing climate change requires a concerted effort from all sectors of society, from individuals and communities to governments and businesses. Throughout this guide, we have explored a variety of strategies and actions that individuals can take to make a meaningful impact on climate change and promote sustainability in their daily lives and communities.

From reducing carbon emissions and adopting sustainable consumption habits to advocating for policy change and engaging in collective action, there are countless ways for individuals to contribute to the fight against climate change. By taking action, raising awareness, and inspiring others to join the cause, individuals can become agents of positive change and help build a more sustainable future for future generations.

However, addressing climate change also requires systemic change and collective action on a global scale. While individual actions are necessary, they must be complemented by policy changes, investments in clean energy and infrastructure, and international cooperation to effectively mitigate the impacts of climate change and promote resilience in the face of its consequences.

As we progress, it's crucial to maintain our focus on climate action, amplify the voices of marginalized communities, and collaborate toward building a fairer, more equitable, and sustainable world for everyone. Through individual efforts, we can harness the significant impact of collective action, building upon the momentum of grassroots movements and global initiatives to address the challenges of climate change and forge a better future for ourselves and future generations. Together, our actions can effect change.

The time for action is now; urgency is paramount!

If you found this book helpful, we would appreciate it if you left a favorable review on Amazon!

References

- Anderson, L., & Anderson, L. (2023, December 28). *Revealing the top Tree-Planting nation.* Riveal. https://riveal.pt/revealing-the-top-treeplanting-nation/
- *Answers to: Remote sensing is a example of an ICT application for climate change observation.* (2023, May 3). Class Ace. https://www.classace.io/answers/remote-sensing-is-a-example-of-an-ict-application-for-climate-change-observation
- Charlotte. (2023, May 30). *Book Review: The more or less Definitive Guide to Self-Care.* The Roundtable. https://goroundtable.com/blog/book-review-the-more-or-less-definite-guide-to-self-care/
- *Dr. R.K. Pachauri.* (n.d.). https://www.rkpachauri.org/
- González, B. (2021, November 9). Data management and a custom educational model - key factors in post-COVID university education. *UOC.* https://www.uoc.edu/en/news/2021/304-post-COVID-university
- *Goodwall: the app for Gen Z to level up their skills.* (n.d.). Goodwall. https://www.goodwall.io/posts/climate-change-refers-to-longterm-ffa0f3e6
- Khadka, C., Upadhyaya, A., Edwards-Jonášová, M., Dhungana, N., Baral, S., & Cudlin, P. (2022). Differential Impact Analysis for Climate Change Adaptation: A Case Study from Nepal. *Sustainability, 14*(16), 9825. https://doi.org/10.3390/su14169825
- *Mozambicans rebuild after deadly Cyclone Freddy - Mozambique.* (2023,

August 16). Relief Web. https://reliefweb.int/report/mozambique/moz ambicans-rebuild-after-deadly-cyclone-freddy

- Pawar, M. (2023, June 15). *Unlocking entrepreneurial success: The power of setting clear expectations - Mohit Pawar.com*. Mohit Pawar.com. https://m ohitpawar.com/set-clear-expectations/
- *Sadam jutt's writes*. (2023, July 29). https://www.sadamwrites.com/searc h?updated-max=2023-07-29T09:27:00-07:00&max-results=5
- Sayings, F. Q. &. (n.d.). *Top 15 Pachauri Quotes & Sayings*. https://quotess ayings.net/topics/pachauri/
- Schulz, K. B. (2015). Information flooding. *Indiana Law Review, 48*(3), 755. https://doi.org/10.18060/4806.0011
- *Sunak to announce £15bn green savings bonds*. (2021, June 30). Good With Money. https://good-with-money.com/2021/06/30/sunak-to-announc e-15bn-green-savings-bonds/
- The POP Movement. (2024, April 29). *Home - the POP Movement - Protect our Planet (POP), Youth inspired by knowledge*. https://thepopmovement.o rg/
- *The world counts*. (n.d.). https://www.theworldcounts.com/challenges/p eople-and-poverty/hunger-and-obesity/food-waste-statistics
- *Yash Sinha | Vocal*. (n.d.). Vocal. https://vocal.media/authors/yash-sinha

Book 2

CLIMATE SERIES

Simple Steps to Sustainability
A Workbook to Guide Individual Climate Action

by
Dr. Ash Pachauri & Dr. Saroj Pachauri

Simple Steps to Sustainability: A Workbook to Guide Individual Climate Action

This workbook is designed to help individuals take practical steps toward addressing climate change and promoting sustainability in their daily lives and communities. Each chapter corresponds to a key theme explored in the main book, **"Small Steps, Big Impact: A Simple Guide to Individual Action and Collective Impact to Tackle Climate Change."** Use this workbook to track your progress, set goals, and reflect on your journey toward positively impacting the environment.

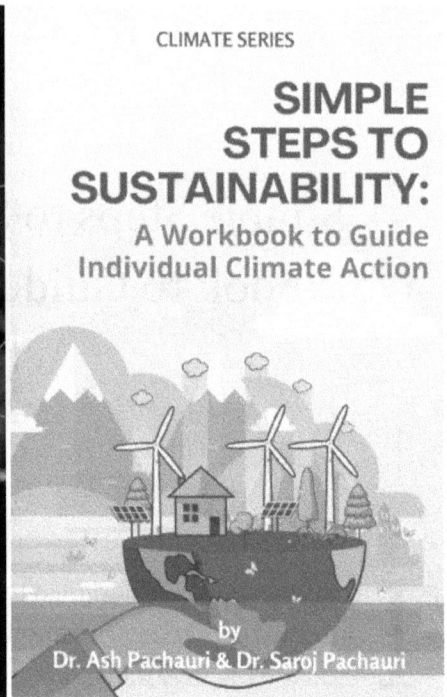

Key Features

Interactive Exercises: Engage with thought-provoking activities that help you understand the science of climate change, calculate your carbon footprint, and set realistic goals for reducing your environmental impact.

Practical Strategies: Discover actionable steps to enhance energy efficiency, adopt sustainable consumption habits, and make eco-friendly dietary choices.

Community Engagement: Learn how to advocate for climate action, organize community events, and participate in collective efforts to create a more sustainable world.

Personal and Community Resilience: Develop plans to build resilience against climate impacts for yourself and your community, ensuring long-term sustainability and preparedness.

Reflection and Goal Setting: Reflect on your journey, track your progress, and set achievable goals that align with your commitment to environmental action.

Who Is This Workbook For?

This workbook is ideal for all responsible citizens of our planet who want to take action against climate change. Whether you are a student, educator, community leader, activist, or concerned citizen, this workbook offers valuable insights and resources to help you make a positive difference.

What You Will Gain

- A deeper understanding of climate change and its global and local impacts.
- Practical tools to reduce your carbon footprint and promote sustainability in your daily life.
- Strategies for engaging in effective advocacy and community action.
- Enhanced resilience to climate-related challenges, ensuring a sustainable future for you and your community.
- A sense of empowerment and motivation to continue your climate action journey.

Join the Movement

Using "Simple Steps to Sustainability: A Workbook to Guide Individual Climate Action," you are taking a crucial step towards creating a more sustainable and resilient future for yourself and your community. Together, we can significantly impact the fight against climate change. Let's take action and build a better world for ourselves and future generations!

Understanding Climate Change

T he activities below are designed to help understand the science behind climate change.

Activity 1: Research and Reflect

1. Research the basic science of climate change. Summarize what you learned in your own words.

- What are the primary causes of climate change?
- What are the significant impacts of climate change on the environment, biodiversity, and ecosystems?
- What are the impacts of climate change you have experienced? How do they make you feel (anxious, angry, helpless)? What can you do to tackle the impacts of climate change as you experience them?

Reflection

Write a short reflection on how understanding the science of climate change has influenced your perspective on the issue.

Activity 2: Personal Carbon Footprint Calculation

1. Use an online carbon footprint calculator to estimate your carbon footprint.

- What are the primary sources of your carbon emissions?
- What surprised you about your carbon footprint?

Reflection

Identify three areas where you can reduce your carbon footprint. List specific actions you will take in these areas.

Energy Efficiency

The activities below are designed to help audit and assess home energy efficiency.

Activity 1: Home Energy Audit

1. Conduct a basic energy audit of your home.

- Identify areas where you can improve energy efficiency (e.g., insulation, lighting, appliances).
- Create a checklist of energy-saving actions you can implement.

Reflection

What changes will you make to reduce energy consumption in your home? How will these changes impact your carbon footprint?

Activity 2: Renewable Energy Options

1. Research renewable energy options available in your area.

- What types of renewable energy are most accessible to you (e.g., solar, wind, geothermal)?
- What are the potential costs and benefits of switching to renewable energy sources within your home and living space?

Reflection

What steps can you take to transition to renewable energy sources? Are there any barriers you need to overcome?

Reducing Carbon Footprint

T he activities below are designed to measure the individual carbon footprint and how to reduce it.

Activity 1: Sustainable Transportation

1. Track your transportation habits for one week.

- How often do you use a car, bike, public transportation, or walk?
- Calculate the carbon emissions associated with your transportation choices.

Reflection

What changes can you make to reduce your transportation-related carbon emissions? Set a goal for incorporating more sustainable transportation methods into your routine.

Activity 2: Dietary Choices

1. Keep a food diary for one week, noting the types of food you consume.

- How often do you eat meat, dairy, plant-based foods, and locally sourced products?
- Research the carbon footprint of different foods.

Reflection

Identify three dietary changes you can make to reduce your carbon footprint. How will these changes benefit the environment?

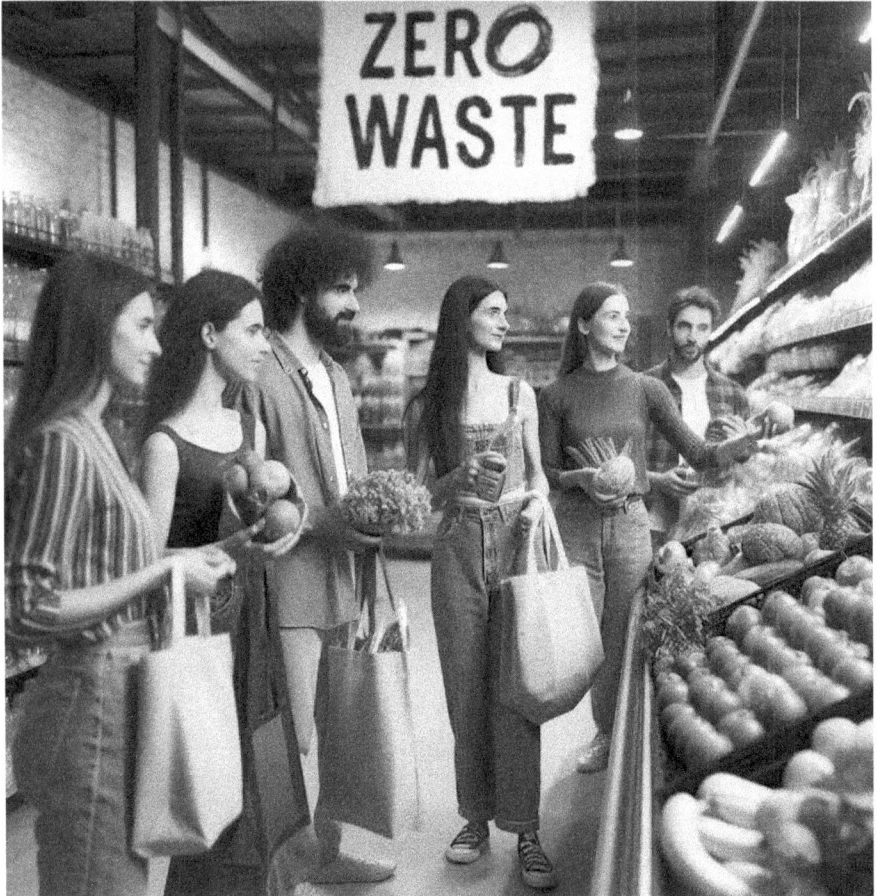

Sustainable Consumption

T he activities below are designed to help understand sustainable consumption practices can protect our planet.

Activity 1: Eco-Labels and Certifications

1. Research common eco-labels and certifications for sustainable products (e.g., Fair Trade, USDA Organic).

- Choose a product you regularly purchase and find a sustainable alternative.
- Compare the environmental impact of the two products.

Reflection

How can you incorporate more eco-friendly products into your shopping habits? What criteria will you use to make more sustainable choices?

Activity 2: Waste Reduction Plan

1. Conduct a waste audit of your household.

- Categorize your waste (e.g., recyclables, compostable, landfill).
- Identify areas where you can refuse, reduce, reuse, and recycle more effectively.

Reflection

Create a waste reduction plan for your household. What steps will you take to minimize waste and increase recycling?

Advocacy and Community Engagement

T he activities below are designed to support climate advocacy and build community engagement.

Activity 1: Write to Your Elected Officials

1. Draft a letter or email to your local or national elected officials.

- Express your concerns about climate change and suggest specific actions they can take.
- Use facts and personal stories to make your case.

Reflection

How can you stay engaged with your elected officials and continue advocating climate action? What other advocacy methods can you explore?

Activity 2: Organize a Community Event

1. Plan a community event focused on climate action (e.g., a clean-up day or educational workshop).

- Outline the goals, activities, and logistics of the event.
- Identify potential partners and resources needed.

Reflection

What impact do you hope to achieve with your event? How can you encourage more people to get involved in climate action in your community?

Investing in the Future

The activities below are designed to support individuals to make green and clean investment choices.

Activity 1: Sustainable Investment Research

1. Research sustainable investment options such as green bonds or sustainable impact investing.

- Choose one investment option and analyze its potential environmental and financial benefits.
- Consider how this investment aligns with your values.

Reflection

How can you align your financial investments with your sustainability goals? How can you encourage others to consider sustainable investing?

Activity 2: Support Local Green Businesses

1. Identify local businesses that prioritize sustainability.

- Visit or contact these businesses to learn more about their practices.
- Choose one business to support and reflect on why you chose them.

Reflection

How can supporting green businesses contribute to a more sustainable local economy? How can you support sustainability through your spending habits and consumption choices?

Education and Awareness

The activities below are designed to help promote climate education and awareness.

Activity 1: Create Educational Content

1. Develop educational content about climate change (e.g., a blog post, video, infographic).

- Choose a specific aspect of climate change to focus on.
- Research and present the information in an engaging and accessible way to share with your friends, family, and community (e.g., via social media or a website).

Reflection

How can you use your skills, accessible media, and platforms to raise awareness about climate change? What impact do you hope to achieve with your educational content?

Activity 2: Host a Workshop or Presentation

1. Plan and host a workshop or presentation on climate change and sustainability (see attached workshop outline, which you may customize to suit your needs and context).

- Identify your audience and tailor your content to their interests and needs.
- Include interactive elements to engage participants.
- Encourage participants to explore climate actions they can take (see

attached guide to individual climate action).

Reflection

What did you learn from hosting the workshop or presentation? How can you continue to educate and inspire others to take climate action?

Workshop:

Inspiring Climate Action: Practical Steps for Sustainable Living

Overview

"Inspiring Climate Action: Practical Steps for Sustainable Living" is an interactive workshop designed to provide participants with the knowledge, tools, and inspiration to take meaningful action against climate change. This workshop combines educational content, practical activities, and collaborative discussions to help individuals understand the impact of their choices and empower them to contribute to a more sustainable future.

Objectives

- Educate participants on the science and impacts of climate change.
- Provide practical strategies for reducing personal and community carbon footprints.
- Foster a sense of community and collective action among participants.
- Empower individuals to advocate for policy changes and engage in climate advocacy.

Agenda

1. Introduction and Icebreaker (15 minutes)

- Welcome and introduction to the workshop.
- Icebreaker activity to encourage participant interaction and engagement.

2. Understanding Climate Change (30 minutes)

- Presentation on the science of climate change, its causes, and effects.
- Discussion on the global and local impacts of climate change.

3. Reducing Your Carbon Footprint (45 minutes)

- Interactive session on practical ways to reduce carbon emissions in daily life, including energy efficiency, sustainable transportation, and waste reduction.
- Activity: Personal carbon footprint calculation and goal-setting.

4. Sustainable Consumption and Dietary Choices (30 minutes)

- Presentation on the environmental impact of consumer choices and food consumption.
- Activity: Identify sustainable products and plan eco-friendly meals.

5. Advocacy and Community Engagement (45 minutes)

- Discussion on the importance of advocacy and collective action.
- Activity: Draft letters to elected officials and plan community events.

6. Building Resilience (30 minutes)

- Presentation on personal and community resilience to climate impacts.
- Activity: Creating personal and community resilience plans.

7. Group Activity: Organizing a Climate Action Campaign (45 minutes)

- Collaborative exercise to plan a climate action campaign.
- Participants will work in groups to outline goals, strategies, and action steps.

8. Reflection and Next Steps (30 minutes)

- Participants share their reflections on the workshop and personal commitments to climate action.
- Discussion on how to stay engaged and continue making a difference.

9. Q&A and Closing Remarks (15 minutes)

- Open the floor for questions and answers.
- Summary of key takeaways and closing remarks.

Materials to be Provided:

- Workbook: **"Simple Steps to Sustainability: A Workbook to Guide Individual Climate Action.**
- Carbon footprint calculators and tracking sheets.
- List of sustainable products and resources.
- Templates for advocacy letters and community event planning.

Who Should Attend?

This workshop is ideal for individuals passionate about tackling climate change, including students, educators, community leaders, activists, and anyone looking to impact the environment positively. No prior knowledge is required; it is just a willingness to learn and take action.

Outcomes

By the end of the workshop, participants will:

- Have a strong understanding of climate change and its impacts.
- Understand practical strategies to reduce their carbon footprint and promote sustainability.
- Feel empowered to engage in climate advocacy and community action.
- Have created actionable plans for personal and community resilience.

Join us for this transformative workshop and become a part of the solution to climate change. Together, we can make a difference!

Climate Change: What Can I Do?

Practical Climate Actions

Individuals can significantly impact climate change by adopting various actions in their daily lives.

Here are some practical climate actions one can take:

Reducing Carbon Footprint

1. Transportation

- Use public transportation, bike, or walk instead of driving.
- Carpool or use ride-sharing services.
- Opt for electric or hybrid vehicles.
- Limit air travel and choose direct flights when possible.

2. Energy Consumption

- Switch to renewable energy sources for your home, such as solar or wind power.
- Install energy-efficient appliances and light bulbs.
- Use programmable thermostats to reduce energy use.
- Insulate your home to maintain temperature and avoid energy losses due to poor insulation.

3. Diet

- Reduce meat and dairy consumption, especially beef and lamb.
- Eat more plant-based foods and locally sourced produce.
- Avoid food waste by planning meals and using leftovers.

Sustainable Living

4. Waste Reduction

- Recycle and compost waste.
- Avoid single-use plastics; use reusable bags, bottles, and containers.
- Buy products with minimal packaging.

5. Water Conservation

- Install low-flow showerheads and faucets.
- Turn off faucets rather than leaving them running when water is not in use (for example, brushing, shaving, or in the shower).
- Fix leaks promptly.
- Use a water-efficient washing machine and dishwasher.
- Collect and use rainwater for gardening.

Supporting Sustainable Practices

6. Consumer Choices

- Support companies with sustainable and ethical practices.
- Buy second-hand or high-quality, durable products.
- Choose eco-friendly clothing brands.
- Avoid fast fashion.

7. Advocacy and Education

- Educate yourself and others about climate change and sustainability.
- Support and vote for policies and leaders that prioritize climate action.
- Participate in or donate to environmental organizations.
- Advocate for sustainability initiatives in your community.

Natural Resource Management

8. Gardening and Agriculture

- Plant trees and support reforestation projects.
- Grow your food or support local organic farmers.
- Use sustainable gardening practices like composting and xeriscaping.

Technology and Innovation

9. Adopt Green Technologies

- Use energy-efficient electronics.
- Invest in smart home technologies that save energy.
- Support technological innovations aimed at reducing emissions.

By integrating these actions into daily life, individuals can contribute to a collective effort to combat climate change and promote a more sustainable future.

Building Resilience

The activities below are designed to help strengthen individual and community climate resilience.

Activity 1: Personal Resilience Plan

1. Assess your resilience to climate-related impacts (e.g., extreme weather, water shortages).

- Identify areas where you can improve your preparedness and adaptability.
- Create a plan to enhance your resilience.

Reflection

How can building personal resilience help you cope with climate change impacts? What steps will you take to implement your resilience plan?

Activity 2: Community Resilience Project

1. Develop a project to enhance community resilience to climate change.

- Identify a specific climate-related risk in your community (e.g., flooding, heatwaves).

- Outline a project that addresses this risk and engages community members.

Reflection

How can you collaborate with others to build community resilience? What resources and partnerships will you need to implement your project successfully?

The Power of Collective Action

The activities below are designed to help build collective climate action.

Activity 1: Join a Climate Action Group

1. Research local, national, or international climate action groups and organizations.

- Choose one group to join and get involved with their activities.
- Participate in meetings, events, and campaigns.

Reflection

How can being part of a climate action group increase your impact? What have you learned from working with others towards a common goal?

Activity 2: Organize a Collective Action Campaign

1. Plan and organize a campaign to address a specific climate issue.

- Define the campaign's goals, target audience, and critical messages.
- Develop a strategy for outreach, engagement, and action. What do you hope to achieve as a result of the action taken?

Reflection

What challenges did you encounter while organizing the campaign? How can you overcome these challenges and strengthen future collective action efforts? How can you sustain the efforts you have initiated?

Conclusion

C ongratulations on completing the "Individual Climate Action" workbook! Reflect on your journey and the progress you have made. Identify areas where you can continue to grow, take action, and celebrate your contributions to creating a more sustainable and resilient future.

Final Reflection

Write a reflection on your overall experience using this workbook. How has it influenced your understanding of climate change and your role in addressing it? What are your next steps in continuing your climate action journey?

Climate Action Trivia Quiz 1

Q uestion 1

Which of the following is the most effective way for an individual to reduce their carbon footprint?

a) Recycling plastics
b) Reducing meat consumption
c) Using energy-efficient light bulbs
d) Carpooling

Question 2

What is the term for the measure of the amount of carbon dioxide emissions for which an individual or organization is responsible?

a) Carbon Tax
b) Carbon Footprint
c) Carbon Credit
d) Carbon Neutrality

Question 3

Which sector is the largest contributor to global greenhouse gas emissions?

a) Agriculture

b) Industry

c) Transportation

d) Energy Production

Question 4

Which of the following actions can governments take to encourage renewable energy use?

a) Subsidies for fossil fuels

b) Implementing a carbon tax

c) Reducing regulations on oil drilling

d) Providing tax breaks for gasoline

Question 5

What is "Earth Hour"?

a) An hour dedicated to cleaning up local parks

b) A global event where people turn off their lights for one hour

c) A time when people plant trees

d) A day for recycling electronics

Question 6

Which of the following is NOT a renewable energy source?

a) Solar power

b) Wind power

c) Nuclear power

d) Hydroelectric power

Question 7

What international agreement aims to limit global warming to well below 2 degrees Celsius above pre-industrial levels?

a) Kyoto Protocol

b) Montreal Protocol

c) Paris Agreement

d) Doha Amendment

Question 8

Which everyday habit can significantly reduce water waste?

a) Taking shorter showers

b) Watering lawns every day

c) Washing clothes in hot water

d) Keeping the tap running while brushing teeth

Question 9

What is a "carbon offset"?

a) A reduction in emissions of carbon dioxide or other greenhouse gases to compensate for emissions made elsewhere

b) A tax imposed on companies based on their carbon emissions

c) A method for capturing and storing carbon dioxide from the atmosphere

d) A mandatory reduction target set by the government for carbon emissions

Question 10

Which type of diet has the lowest carbon footprint?

a) Omnivorous diet

b) Vegetarian diet

c) Vegan diet

d) Pescatarian diet

Answers, explanations, and references to Climate Action Trivia Quiz 1

Question 1

Answer: b) Reducing meat consumption

Explanation: Livestock production is a significant source of green-house gases, including methane. Reducing meat consumption, especially beef, can lower an individual's carbon footprint significantly.

Reference: [Environmental Impact of Meat Production]
  (https://www.theguardian.com/environment/2018/jul/19/avoiding-meat-and-dairy-is-single-biggest-way-to-reduce-your-impact-on-earth)

Question 2

Answer: b) Carbon Footprint

Explanation: A carbon footprint is the total amount of greenhouse gases (including carbon dioxide and methane) that are emitted by an individual, organization, event, or product.

Reference: [Carbon Footprint](https://www.nature.org/en-us/get-involved/how-to-help/carbon-footprint-calculator/)

Question 3

Answer: d) Energy Production

Explanation: The energy sector, including electricity and heat production, is the largest source of global greenhouse gas emissions due to the burning of fossil fuels like coal, oil, and gas.

Reference: [Global Greenhouse Gas Emissions Data] (https://www.epa.gov/ghgem issions/global-greenhouse-gas-emissions-data)

Question 4

Answer: b) Implementing a carbon tax

Explanation: A carbon tax puts a price on carbon emissions, incentivizing businesses and individuals to reduce their carbon footprint and invest in renewable energy sources.

Reference: [Carbon Tax Basics](https://www.c2es.org/content/carbon-tax-basics/)

Question 5

Answer: b) A global event where people turn off their lights for one hour

Explanation: Earth Hour is an annual event organized by the World Wildlife Fund (WWF), encouraging individuals, communities, and businesses to turn off non-essential electric lights for one hour to raise awareness about climate change.

Reference: [Earth Hour](https://www.earthhour.org/)

Question 6

Answer: c) Nuclear power

Explanation: While nuclear power is a low-carbon energy source, it is not renewable because it relies on uranium, which is a finite resource.

Reference: [Renewable Energy Explained](https://www.eia.gov/energyexplained/r

enewable-sources/)

Question 7

Answer: c) Paris Agreement

Explanation: The Paris Agreement is an international treaty adopted in 2015, aiming to limit global warming to well below 2 degrees Celsius, with efforts to limit it to 1.5 degrees Celsius.

Reference: [Paris Agreement](https://unfccc.int/process-and-meetings/the-paris-agreement/the-paris-agreement)

Question 8

Answer: a) Taking shorter showers

Explanation: Shortening the duration of showers is an effective way to reduce water consumption and the energy needed to heat the water.

Reference: [Water Conservation Tips](https://www.epa.gov/watersense/how-we-use-water)

Question 9

Answer: a) A reduction in emissions of carbon dioxide or other greenhouse gases to compensate for emissions made elsewhere

Explanation: Carbon offsets are credits purchased to fund projects that reduce or remove greenhouse gases from the atmosphere, compensating for emissions made elsewhere.

Reference: [Carbon Offsets](https://www.green-e.org/certified-resources/carbon-o

ffsets)

Question 10

Answer: c) Vegan diet

Explanation: A vegan diet typically has the lowest carbon footprint because it eliminates all animal products, which are generally more resource-intensive and produce more greenhouse gases than plant-based foods.

Reference: [Environmental Benefits of a Vegan Diet] (https://www.oxfordmartin.ox.ac.uk/news/201603_peter_scarborough_diet/)

Feel free to use this quiz along with the explanations and references to enhance learning and awareness about climate action!

Climate Action Trivia Quiz 2

Q**uestion 1**

What is the best way to reduce energy consumption at home?

a) Leaving electronics on standby

b) Using energy-efficient appliances

c) Keeping lights on all day

d) Using single-use batteries

Question 2

Which form of transportation generally has the lowest carbon footprint?

a) Driving a gasoline car

b) Flying in an airplane

c) Biking

d) Taking a cruise ship

Question 3

What type of waste can be composted at home?

a) Plastic bottles

b) Food scraps

c) Metal cans

d) Glass jars

Question 4

How can individuals reduce water usage when gardening?
  a) Watering plants during the hottest part of the day
  b) Using a hose without a nozzle
  c) Installing a rain barrel
  d) Planting non-native species

Question 5

What is a simple way to reduce paper waste?
  a) Printing out all emails
  b) Using reusable cloth napkins
  c) Using disposable plates
  d) Using single-use paper towels

Question 6

Which household activity uses the most water?
  a) Doing laundry
  b) Washing dishes by hand
  c) Taking a bath
  d) Flushing the toilet

Question 7

What is the impact of reducing food waste on the environment?
  a) No significant impact
  b) Increases greenhouse gas emissions
  c) Reduces methane emissions from landfills

d) Increases water usage

Question 8

Which is a better choice for the environment:
   a) Buying new products
   b) Reusing and repurposing items
   c) Using single-use products
   d) Frequently updating to the latest technology

Question 9

What is an effective way to reduce plastic pollution?
   a) Using plastic bags
   b) Avoiding plastic straws
   c) Buying bottled water
   d) Using plastic utensils

Question 10

Which type of light bulb is the most energy-efficient?
   a) Incandescent
   b) Halogen
   c) CFL (Compact Fluorescent Light)
   d) LED (Light Emitting Diode)

Answers, explanations, and references to Climate Action Trivia Quiz 2

Question 1

Answer: b) Using energy-efficient appliances

Explanation: Energy-efficient appliances consume less electricity, reducing overall energy consumption and utility bills. They are designed to use technology that conserves energy without compromising performance.

Reference: [Energy Star: Energy Efficient Products](https://www.energystar.gov/products)

Question 2

Answer: c) Biking

Explanation: Biking has the lowest carbon footprint because it does not rely on fossil fuels and emits no greenhouse gases. It is a sustainable mode of transportation that also offers health benefits.

Reference: [European Cyclists' Federation: Cycle More Often 2 Cool Down the Planet](https://ecf.com/sites/ecf.com/files/ECF_CO2_WEB.pdf)

Question 3

Answer: b) Food scraps

Explanation: Food scraps, along with other organic materials like yard waste, can be composted at home. Composting helps reduce landfill waste and creates nutrient-rich soil for gardening.

Reference: [EPA: Composting at Home](https://www.epa.gov/recycle/composting-home)

Question 4

Answer: c) Installing a rain barrel

Explanation: Installing a rain barrel allows individuals to collect and store rainwater, which can then be used to water plants. This conserves tap water and reduces water bills.

Reference: [EPA: WaterSense - Outdoor Water Use in the United States](https://www.epa.gov/watersense/outdoor)

Question 5

Answer: b) Using reusable cloth napkins

Explanation: Using reusable cloth napkins reduces the need for disposable paper products, thus reducing paper waste. This helps save trees and decreases the volume of waste sent to landfills.

Reference: [EPA: Reducing Waste: What You Can Do](https://www.epa.gov/recycle/reducing-waste-what-you-can-do)

Question 6

Answer: d) Flushing the toilet

Explanation: Flushing the toilet typically uses the most water in a household. Installing low-flow toilets or using water-saving devices can significantly reduce water usage.

Reference: [USGS: Water Use in the United States](https://www.usgs.gov/special-topics/water-science-school/science/water-use-united-states)

Question 7

Answer: c) Reduces methane emissions from landfills

Explanation: Reducing food waste decreases the amount of organic waste that decomposes in landfills, which in turn reduces methane emissions, a potent greenhouse gas.

Reference: [FAO: Food Wastage Footprint](http://www.fao.org/nr/sustainability/food-loss-and-waste/en/)

Question 8

Answer: b) Reusing and repurposing items

Explanation: Reusing and repurposing items reduces the demand for new products, which decreases resource extraction and production emissions. It also minimizes waste generation.

Reference: [EPA: Reduce, Reuse, Recycle](https://www.epa.gov/recycle/reducing-and-reusing-basics)

Question 9

Answer: b) Avoiding plastic straws

Explanation: Avoiding single-use plastic straws (and other single-use plastics) helps reduce plastic pollution. These items are often not recycled and can harm marine life when they end up in oceans.

Reference: [National Geographic: The Trouble with Plastic Straws](https://www.nationalgeographic.com/environment/article/are-plastic-straws-bad-for-the-environment)

Question 10

Answer: d) LED (Light Emitting Diode)

Explanation: LED bulbs are the most energy-efficient, using up to 80% less energy than traditional incandescent bulbs. They also have a longer lifespan, reducing waste and energy consumption.

Reference: [Energy.gov: LED Lighting](https://www.energy.gov/energysaver/led-lighting)

Feel free to use this quiz along with the explanations and references to promote awareness and action for individual climate action!

Climate Action Trivia Quiz 3

Question 1

What is the primary cause of global warming?

    a) Volcanic eruptions

b) Solar flares

c) Human activities

d) Natural climate cycles

Question 2

Which greenhouse gas is most commonly produced by human activities?

a) Methane

b) Nitrous oxide

c) Carbon dioxide

d) Chlorofluorocarbons (CFCs)

Question 3

What percentage of the Earth's surface is covered by oceans, which play a crucial role in regulating the climate?

a) 50%

b) 60%

c) 70%

d) 80%

Question 4

Which renewable energy source generates the most electricity world-wide?
a) Solar power
b) Wind power
c) Hydropower
d) Geothermal power

Question 5

What is the effect of deforestation on climate change?
a) Reduces greenhouse gases
b) Increases greenhouse gases
c) No effect on greenhouse gases
d) Only affects local climate

Question 6

What international initiative encourages cities to publicly disclose their environmental impact and take action to reduce greenhouse gases?
a) C40 Cities Climate Leadership Group
b) Kyoto Protocol
c) Intergovernmental Panel on Climate Change (IPCC)
d) Global Covenant of Mayors for Climate & Energy

Question 7

What is the primary aim of the UN's Sustainable Development Goal

(SDG) 13?

a) Ensure access to clean water

b) Combat climate change and its impacts

c) Promote affordable and clean energy

d) End poverty in all its forms

Question 8

Which country is the largest emitter of carbon dioxide as of recent data?

a) United States

b) India

c) China

d) Russia

Question 9

What is the term for the warming of the Earth due to trapped heat from the sun in the atmosphere?

a) Ozone depletion

b) Greenhouse effect

c) Acid rain

d) Albedo effect

Question 10

Which practice helps in reducing the urban heat island effect in cities?

a) Increasing asphalt roads

b) Planting more trees and green spaces

c) Constructing more buildings

d) Removing parks and gardens

Answers, Explanations, and References

Question 1

Answer: c) Human activities

Explanation: Human activities, such as burning fossil fuels, deforestation, and industrial processes, release large amounts of greenhouse gases into the atmosphere, leading to global warming.

Reference: [NASA: Causes of Climate Change](https://climate.nasa.gov/causes/)

Question 2

Answer: c) Carbon dioxide

Explanation: Carbon dioxide (CO2) is the most significant greenhouse gas released by human activities, primarily from burning fossil fuels for energy and transportation.

Reference: [EPA: Overview of Greenhouse Gases](https://www.epa.gov/ghgemissions/overview-greenhouse-gases)

Question 3

Answer: c) 70%

Explanation: Approximately 70% of the Earth's surface is covered by oceans, which absorb heat and carbon dioxide, playing a crucial role in regulating the global climate.

Reference: [NOAA: How much of the Earth is covered by water?](https://oceanservice.noaa.gov/facts/oceanwater.html)

Question 4

Answer: c) Hydropower

Explanation: Hydropower, or hydroelectric power, generates the most electricity worldwide among renewable energy sources, utilizing the energy of flowing water.

Reference: [International Hydropower Association](https://www.hydropower.org/what-we-do)

Question 5

Answer: b) Increases greenhouse gases

Explanation: Deforestation increases greenhouse gas emissions by reducing the number of trees that can absorb carbon dioxide. The clearing and burning of forests also release stored carbon.

Reference: [WWF: Deforestation and Forest Degradation](https://www.worldwildlife.org/threats/deforestation-and-forest-degradation)

Question 6

Answer: a) C40 Cities Climate Leadership Group

Explanation: The C40 Cities Climate Leadership Group is a network of the world's megacities committed to addressing climate change by sharing knowledge and best practices.

Reference: [C40 Cities](https://www.c40.org/)

Question 7

Answer: b) Combat climate change and its impacts

Explanation: Sustainable Development Goal (SDG) 13 focuses on taking urgent action to combat climate change and its impacts.

Reference: [United Nations: Goal 13](https://sdgs.un.org/goals/goal13)

Question 8

Answer: c) China

Explanation: China is currently the largest emitter of carbon dioxide, primarily due to its large population and rapid industrialization.

Reference: [Global Carbon Atlas](http://www.globalcarbonatlas.org/en/CO 2-emissions)

Question 9

Answer: b) Greenhouse effect

Explanation: The greenhouse effect is the warming of the Earth's surface and lower atmosphere caused by the presence of greenhouse gases, which trap heat from the sun.

Reference: [National Geographic: Greenhouse Effect](https://www.nationalgeogra phic.org/encyclopedia/greenhouse-effect/)

Question 10

Answer: b) Planting more trees and green spaces

Explanation: Increasing urban green spaces, such as parks and trees, helps reduce the urban heat island effect by providing shade and cooling through evapotranspiration.

Reference: [EPA: Heat Island Effect](https://www.epa.gov/heatislands)

Feel free to use this quiz along with the explanations and references to promote climate change awareness and action!

Climate Action Trivia Quiz 4

Question 1

What percentage of global greenhouse gas emissions is attributed to agriculture?

a) 10%

b) 14%

c) 24%

d) 30%

Question 2

Which international agreement, signed in 1997, aimed to reduce greenhouse gas emissions but was later replaced by the Paris Agreement?

a) Kyoto Protocol

b) Montreal Protocol

c) Copenhagen Accord

d) Doha Amendment

Question 3

What is the primary greenhouse gas emitted through human activities?

a) Methane

b) Nitrous oxide

c) Carbon dioxide

d) Chlorofluorocarbons (CFCs)

Question 4

Which sector is the largest source of methane emissions?

a) Transportation

b) Agriculture

c) Industry

d) Waste management

Question 5

What is the term for the gradual increase in the Earth's average surface temperature due to human activities?

a) Global cooling

b) Global warming

c) Ozone depletion

d) Acid rain

Question 6

Which country is leading in renewable energy production, particularly in wind and solar power?

a) Germany

b) China

c) United States

d) India

Question 7

What is "carbon neutrality"?

a) Emitting zero carbon dioxide

b) Balancing emitted carbon with carbon offsets

c) Reducing carbon emissions by half

d) Completely avoiding fossil fuels

Question 8

What natural process absorbs about 25% of human-caused carbon dioxide emissions annually?

a) Ocean absorption

b) Photosynthesis in plants

c) Soil sequestration

d) Methane oxidation

Question 9

Which ecosystem is considered a major carbon sink, absorbing more carbon dioxide than it releases?

a) Deserts

b) Grasslands

c) Forests

d) Urban areas

Question 10

What individual action can significantly reduce household carbon emissions?

a) Using a gas stove

b) Installing energy-efficient windows

c) Washing clothes in hot water

d) Driving a gasoline-powered car

Answers, explanations, and references to Climate Action Trivia Quiz 3

Question 1

Answer: c) 24%

Explanation: Agriculture is responsible for approximately 24% of global greenhouse gas emissions, primarily from methane and nitrous oxide from livestock and fertilizers.

Reference: [FAO: Greenhouse Gas Emissions from Agriculture](http://www.fao.or g/news/story/en/item/216137/icode/)

Question 2

Answer: a) Kyoto Protocol

Explanation: The Kyoto Protocol was an international treaty adopted in 1997 that committed its parties to reduce greenhouse gas emissions, which was later replaced by the more inclusive and flexible Paris Agreement in 2015.

Reference: [UNFCCC: Kyoto Protocol](https://unfccc.int/kyoto_protocol)

Question 3

Answer: c) Carbon dioxide

Explanation: Carbon dioxide (CO2) is the most significant greenhouse gas emitted through human activities, primarily from burning fossil fuels for energy and transportation.

Reference: [EPA: Overview of Greenhouse Gases](https://www.epa.gov/ghgemissio ns/overview-greenhouse-gases)

Question 4

Answer: b) Agriculture

Explanation: Agriculture is the largest source of methane emissions, mainly from enteric fermentation in ruminant animals and rice paddies.

Reference: [EPA: Methane Emissions](https://www.epa.gov/ghgemissions/overview-greenhouse-gases#methane)

Question 5

Answer: b) Global warming

Explanation: Global warming refers to the long-term increase in Earth's average surface temperature due to human activities, particularly the emission of greenhouse gases.

Reference: [NASA: Global Warming](https://climate.nasa.gov/causes/)

Question 6

Answer: b) China

Explanation: China leads the world in renewable energy production, particularly in wind and solar power, investing heavily in these sectors to reduce its carbon footprint.

Reference: [IEA: China and Renewable Energy](https://www.iea.org/reports/renewables-2020/china)

Question 7

Answer: b) Balancing emitted carbon with carbon offsets

Explanation: Carbon neutrality means achieving a balance between emitting carbon and absorbing carbon from the atmosphere in carbon sinks, often through carbon offsets and renewable energy investments.

Reference: [UNFCCC: What is Carbon Neutrality?](https://unfccc.int/news/what -do-net-zero-and-carbon-neutral-mean)

Question 8

Answer: a) Ocean absorption

Explanation: The oceans absorb about 25% of human-caused carbon dioxide emissions annually, playing a crucial role in mitigating climate change.

Reference: [NOAA: Ocean Carbon Uptake](https://www.noaa.gov/education/reso urce-collections/ocean-coasts/ocean-carbon-uptake)

Question 9

Answer: c) Forests

Explanation: Forests act as major carbon sinks, absorbing more carbon dioxide than they release through photosynthesis and storing carbon in biomass and soils.

Reference: [FAO: Forests and Climate Change](http://www.fao.org/forestry/clima techange/en/)

Question 10

Answer: b) Installing energy-efficient windows

Explanation: Installing energy-efficient windows can significantly reduce household energy use for heating and cooling, thereby reducing carbon emissions.

Reference: [Energy.gov: Energy-efficient Windows](https://www.energy.gov/energysaver/design/windows-doors-and-skylights/energy-efficient-windows)

Feel free to use this quiz along with the explanations and references to enhance understanding and awareness of climate change and climate action!

Climate Action Trivia Quiz 5

Q uestion 1

Which of the following is a significant way to reduce your carbon footprint related to transportation?

a) Driving alone
b) Carpooling
c) Using gasoline-powered vehicles
d) Increasing air travel

Question 2

What is the most energy-efficient way to wash clothes?

a) Washing in hot water
b) Using the dryer
c) Washing in cold water
d) Using a laundromat

Question 3

How can you reduce waste when shopping for groceries?

a) Using plastic bags
b) Buying single-use items
c) Using reusable bags

d) Purchasing individually wrapped items

Question 4

What is the impact of reducing meat consumption on climate change?
   a) No impact
   b) Increases greenhouse gases
   c) Reduces greenhouse gases
   d) Only impacts local pollution

Question 5

Which household activity contributes most to energy use?
   a) Lighting
   b) Cooking
   c) Heating and cooling
   d) Using electronics

Question 6

What is a simple way to conserve water at home?
   a) Taking long showers
   b) Fixing leaky faucets
   c) Watering the lawn daily
   d) Keeping the tap running while brushing teeth

Question 7

What is an effective way to reduce plastic waste?
   a) Using single-use plastic bottles
   b) Avoiding plastic straws
   c) Buying plastic-packaged goods
   d) Using plastic utensils

Question 8

What does "zero waste" mean?
  a) Producing no waste at all
  b) Sending waste to landfills
  c) Recycling most waste
  d) Reducing waste to the minimum and reusing or composting as much as possible

Question 9

How can planting trees help combat climate change?
  a) Trees have no effect on climate
  b) Trees release carbon dioxide
  c) Trees absorb carbon dioxide
  d) Trees only provide shade

Question 10

Which practice is part of sustainable eating?
  a) Wasting food
  b) Eating out frequently
  c) Choosing locally produced food
  d) Eating highly processed food

Answers, Explanations, and References

Question 1

Answer: b) Carpooling

Explanation: Carpooling reduces the number of vehicles on the road,

which in turn reduces greenhouse gas emissions and lowers your carbon footprint.

Reference: [EPA: Reducing Pollution from Vehicles and Engines](https://www.epa. gov/transportation-air-pollution-and-climate-change/what-you-can-do-reduce-p ollution-vehicles-and-engines)

Question 2

Answer: c) Washing in cold water

Explanation: Washing clothes in cold water saves energy because heating water accounts for a significant portion of the energy used in laundry.

Reference: [Energy Star: Clothes Washers](https://www.energystar.gov/products/c lothes_washers)

Question 3

Answer: c) Using reusable bags

Explanation: Using reusable bags reduces the demand for single-use plastic bags, which are a major source of plastic pollution.

Reference: [NRDC: The Problem with Plastic Bags](https://www.nrdc.org/stories/ truth-about-plastic-bag-bans)

Question 4

Answer: c) Reduces greenhouse gases

Explanation: Reducing meat consumption lowers methane emissions

from livestock and decreases the carbon footprint associated with meat production.

Reference: [Environmental Impact of Meat Production](https://www.theguardian.com/environment/2018/jul/19/avoiding-meat-and-dairy-is-single-biggest-way-to-reduce-your-impact-on-earth)

Question 5

Answer: c) Heating and cooling

Explanation: Heating and cooling systems consume the most energy in a typical household, significantly contributing to energy use and carbon emissions.

Reference: [Energy.gov: Home Energy Use](https://www.energy.gov/energysaver/home-energy-use)

Question 6

Answer: b) Fixing leaky faucets

Explanation: Fixing leaky faucets can save a significant amount of water, helping to conserve this precious resource and reduce your water bill.

Reference: [EPA: Fix a Leak Week](https://www.epa.gov/watersense/fix-leak-week)

Question 7

Answer: b) Avoiding plastic straws

Explanation: Avoiding single-use plastic straws reduces plastic waste and helps prevent pollution in oceans and other natural environments.

Reference: [National Geographic: Plastic Pollution](https://www.nationalgeograp hic.com/environment/article/plastic-pollution)

Question 8

Answer: d) Reducing waste to the minimum and reusing or composting as much as possible

Explanation: The zero-waste philosophy aims to minimize waste by reusing, recycling, and composting as much as possible, thereby reducing the amount of waste sent to landfills.

Reference: [Zero Waste International Alliance](http://zwia.org/)

Question 9

Answer: c) Trees absorb carbon dioxide

Explanation: Trees absorb carbon dioxide during photosynthesis, which helps to mitigate the effects of climate change by reducing the amount of CO2 in the atmosphere.

Reference: [Arbor Day Foundation: How Trees Fight Climate Change](https://ww w.arborday.org/trees/climatechange/)

Question 10

Answer: c) Choosing locally produced food

Explanation: Choosing locally produced food reduces the carbon

footprint associated with transporting food over long distances and supports local economies.

Reference: [Sustainable Table: Benefits of Local Food](https://www.sustainabletabl e.org/254/local-regional-food-systems)

Feel free to use this quiz along with the explanations and references to promote awareness and action for individual climate action!

Climate Curiosity About Human Actions Leading to Climate Change and Their Impacts

Fact 1: Fossil Fuel Combustion

Fact: Burning fossil fuels for energy accounts for about 76% of global greenhouse gas emissions.

Explanation: The combustion of coal, oil, and natural gas for electricity and heat production releases significant amounts of CO_2 and other greenhouse gases into the atmosphere. This is the primary driver of climate change.

Reference: EPA: Global Greenhouse Gas Emissions Data

Impact: Global Warming

Impact: The increase in greenhouse gases from burning fossil fuels leads to higher global temperatures, resulting in heatwaves, melting ice caps, and rising sea levels.

Reference: NASA: Global Temperature

Fact 2: Deforestation

Fact: Every year, an area of forest the size of Panama is lost, contributing to about 10% of global carbon emissions.

Explanation: Trees absorb CO2 from the atmosphere. When forests are cleared for agriculture, logging, or development, the stored carbon is released back into the atmosphere, exacerbating global warming.

Reference: WWF: Deforestation and Climate Change

Impact: Loss of Biodiversity

Impact: Deforestation leads to habitat loss, threatening the survival of many species (including humans) and reducing biodiversity, which can disrupt ecosystems and affect human livelihoods.

Reference: National Geographic: Deforestation

Fact 3: Industrial Agriculture

Fact: Agriculture is responsible for about 24% of global greenhouse gas emissions, primarily from livestock, soil management, and rice production.

Explanation: Livestock produce methane during digestion, fertilizers release nitrous oxide, and rice paddies emit methane. These activities contribute significantly to greenhouse gas emissions.

Reference: FAO: Greenhouse Gas Emissions from Agriculture

Impact: Soil Degradation

Impact: Intensive farming practices lead to soil erosion, loss of fertility, and desertification, which reduce agricultural productivity and contribute to food insecurity.

Reference: UNCCD: Soil Degradation

Fact 4: Transportation Emissions

Fact: The transportation sector accounts for about 14% of global greenhouse gas emissions, with cars, trucks, planes, and ships being major contributors.

Explanation: The burning of gasoline and diesel fuels for transportation emits CO_2 and other pollutants. Increasing vehicle numbers and miles traveled exacerbate the problem.

Reference: EPA: Sources of Greenhouse Gas Emissions

Impact: Air Pollution and Health Issues

Impact: Transportation emissions contribute to air pollution, which can cause respiratory and cardiovascular diseases, leading to premature deaths and significant healthcare costs.

Reference: WHO: Ambient Air Pollution

Fact 5: Industrial Processes

Fact: Industrial activities, including cement production and chemical manufacturing, account for about 21% of global greenhouse gas emissions.

Explanation: These industries release CO_2 and other greenhouse gases through energy use and chemical reactions. Cement production alone is responsible for 8% of global CO_2 emissions.

Reference: IEA: Industry Sector CO2 Emissions

Impact: Ocean Acidification

Impact: Increased CO2 levels lead to ocean acidification, which harms marine life, particularly shell-forming organisms like corals and mollusks, affecting marine ecosystems and fisheries.

Reference: NOAA: Ocean Acidification

Fact 6: Waste Management

Fact: Landfills are the third-largest source of human-related methane emissions, contributing to about 11% of global methane emissions.

Explanation: Organic waste in landfills decomposes anaerobically, producing methane, a potent greenhouse gas. Improved waste management practices can significantly reduce these emissions.

Reference: EPA: Global Emissions by Gas

Impact: Methane Emissions

Impact: Methane has a global warming potential 28-36 times greater than CO2 over a 100-year period, making it a significant driver of short-term climate change.

Reference: IPCC: Fifth Assessment Report

Fact 7: Energy Inefficiency

Fact: Buildings account for about 6% of global greenhouse gas emissions due to energy use for heating, cooling, and lighting.

Explanation: Inefficient buildings consume more energy, primarily from fossil fuels, leading to higher greenhouse gas emissions. Improving energy efficiency can significantly reduce these emissions.

Reference: IEA: Buildings

Impact: Increased Energy Demand

Impact: High energy consumption from inefficient buildings increases the demand for fossil fuels, contributing to higher greenhouse gas emissions and exacerbating climate change.

Reference: EPA: Energy and the Environment

Fact 8: Consumerism

Fact: The production and disposal of goods contribute to about 60% of global greenhouse gas emissions, driven by consumer demand for new products.

Explanation: The lifecycle of products—from extraction of raw materials to manufacturing, transportation, and disposal—results in significant greenhouse gas emissions. Reducing consumption and promoting circular economy practices can help mitigate these impacts.

Reference: UNEP: The Emissions Gap Report 2020

Impact: Resource Depletion

Impact: High levels of consumerism lead to over-extraction of natural resources, habitat destruction, and increased waste, which contribute to environmental degradation and climate change.

Reference: Circular Economy: The Benefits

Fact 9: Urbanization

Fact: Urban areas are responsible for about 70% of global CO2 emissions due to high energy consumption and transportation needs.

Explanation: Cities concentrate people, industries, and infrastructure, leading to high energy demand and significant greenhouse gas emissions. Sustainable urban planning and green infrastructure can reduce these emissions.

Reference: UN Habitat: Cities and Climate Change

Impact: Heat Islands

Impact: Urban areas often experience higher temperatures than rural areas due to the heat island effect, which increases energy demand for cooling and exacerbates climate change impacts.

Reference: EPA: Heat Island Effect

These facts and their associated impacts illustrate how various human activities contribute to climate change and highlight the importance of mitigating these effects through sustainable practices and policies.

Climate Curiosity About Individual Action to Protect Our Planet

Fact 1: Energy-Efficient Appliances Save More Than Just Energy

Fact: Replacing an old refrigerator with an Energy Star-certified model can save enough energy to power a new LED TV for over two years.

Explanation: Energy-efficient appliances use advanced technologies to reduce energy consumption, leading to significant savings on utility bills and reducing the overall carbon footprint.

Reference: Energy Star: Refrigerators

Fact 2: Biking Is a Triple Win

Fact: Biking for just 10 kilometers instead of driving can prevent the emission of about 1.3 kilograms of CO_2, save money on fuel, and improve your health.

Explanation: Biking is a zero-emission mode of transport that reduces greenhouse gases, saves money on transportation costs, and offers physical health benefits such as improved cardiovascular health.

Reference: European Cyclists' Federation: Cycle More Often 2 Cool Down the Planet

Fact 3: Composting Transforms Waste into Treasure

Fact: Composting your kitchen and yard waste can divert up to 30% of household waste from landfills.

Explanation: Composting organic waste reduces the amount of material sent to landfills, decreases methane emissions from waste decomposition, and creates nutrient-rich soil for gardening.

Reference: EPA: Composting at Home

Fact 4: Rain Barrels Are an Ancient, Yet Modern Solution

Fact: Rain barrels have been used since ancient times and can save about 1,300 gallons of water during peak summer months.

Explanation: Collecting rainwater using barrels helps conserve water, reduces stormwater runoff, and provides a free water source for gardening and other outdoor uses.

Reference: EPA: WaterSense - Outdoor Water Use in the United States

Fact 5: Reusable Items Can Make a Big Impact

Fact: Using a reusable water bottle can save an average of 156 plastic bottles annually per person.

Explanation: Switching to reusable items like water bottles significantly reduces plastic waste, minimizes environmental pollution, and conserves resources used in the production of single-use plastics.

Reference: NRDC: The Problem with Plastic Bottles

Fact 6: Low-Flow Toilets Make a Splash in Water Conservation

Fact: Installing a low-flow toilet can save up to 13,000 gallons of water per year for a family of four.

Explanation: Low-flow toilets use less water per flush compared to traditional models, significantly reducing household water usage and conserving this vital resource.

Reference: EPA: WaterSense - Toilets

Fact 7: Reducing Food Waste Saves Money and the Planet

Fact: The average family of four can save about $1,500 a year by preventing food waste.

Explanation: Reducing food waste not only conserves resources used in food production but also lowers greenhouse gas emissions from decomposing food in landfills and saves money by making better use of purchased food.

Reference: NRDC: Wasted - How America Is Losing Up to 40 Percent of Its Food from Farm to Fork to Landfill

Fact 8: LED Bulbs Light the Way to Savings

Fact: LED bulbs use at least 75% less energy and last 25 times longer than incandescent lighting.

Explanation: LEDs are highly energy-efficient and have a long lifespan, reducing energy consumption and the frequency of bulb replacements, which lowers environmental impact and costs.

Reference: Energy.gov: LED Lighting

Fact 9: Planting Trees Has Long-Lasting Benefits

Fact: One mature tree can absorb carbon dioxide at a rate of 48 pounds per year, and release enough oxygen back into the atmosphere to support two human beings.

Explanation: Trees play a critical role in mitigating climate change by absorbing CO_2, providing oxygen, and offering other environmental benefits such as cooling urban areas and supporting biodiversity.

Reference: Arbor Day Foundation: Benefits of Trees

Fact 10: Eating Local Reduces Your Carbon "Foodprint"

Fact: Locally grown produce often travels less than 100 miles to reach your plate, compared to 1,500 miles for conventionally sourced food.

Explanation: Eating locally grown food reduces the carbon emissions associated with transporting food over long distances, supports local farmers, and often means fresher, more nutritious produce.

Reference: Sustainable Table: Benefits of Local Food

These facts, explanations, and references can be included to educate and inspire citizens about the impact of individual climate actions.

Climate Curiosity About Individual Action and Household Savings

Fact 1: Energy-Efficient Appliances Save Big Bucks

Fact: Replacing an old refrigerator with an Energy Star-certified model can save you up to $150 per year on energy bills.

Explanation: Energy-efficient appliances use advanced technology to minimize energy consumption, leading to significant savings on utility bills and reduced carbon footprints.

Reference: Energy Star: Refrigerators

Fact 2: LED Bulbs Light the Way to Savings

Fact: Switching to LED light bulbs can save you around $225 per year in energy costs.

Explanation: LED bulbs are highly energy-efficient, using at least 75% less energy than incandescent bulbs and lasting much longer, which reduces energy bills and the need for frequent replacements.

Reference: Energy.gov: LED Lighting

Fact 3: Programmable Thermostats Pay Off

Fact: Using a programmable thermostat can save you up to 10% on heating and cooling costs, which could be about $180 per year for the average household.

Explanation: Programmable thermostats automatically adjust the temperature in your home based on your schedule, reducing unnecessary heating and cooling when you are away or asleep.

Reference: Energy Star: Programmable Thermostats

Fact 4: Low-Flow Fixtures Conserve Water and Money

Fact: Installing low-flow showerheads can save a family of four up to $260 annually on water and energy bills.

Explanation: Low-flow fixtures reduce the amount of water used without compromising performance, leading to savings on both water and energy bills due to reduced water heating.

Reference: EPA: WaterSense - Showerheads

Fact 5: Sealing and Insulating Your Home

Fact: Properly sealing and insulating your home can save up to 20% on heating and cooling costs, which translates to about $200 per year.

Explanation: Sealing leaks and adding insulation keeps your home warmer in the winter and cooler in the summer, reducing the need for excessive heating and cooling.

Reference: Energy Star: Home Sealing

Fact 6: Using a Rain Barrel

Fact: Using a rain barrel can save up to 1,300 gallons of water during peak summer months, reducing your water bill.

Explanation: Rain barrels collect and store rainwater, which can be used for outdoor irrigation, reducing the need to use tap water and lowering water bills.

Reference: EPA: WaterSense - Outdoor Water Use in the United States

Fact 7: Composting Reduces Waste and Saves on Fertilizers

Fact: Composting at home can reduce your household waste by up to 30% and save you money on garden fertilizers.

Explanation: Composting organic waste such as food scraps and yard trimmings reduces the amount of waste sent to landfills and produces nutrient-rich compost that can be used to enhance soil health, eliminating the need for commercial fertilizers.

Reference: EPA: Composting at Home

Fact 8: Reducing Food Waste

Fact: The average family of four can save approximately $1,500 per year by reducing food waste.

Explanation: By planning meals, storing food properly, and using leftovers, households can significantly reduce the amount of food that goes to waste, saving money and reducing the environmental impact of food production and disposal.

Reference: NRDC: Wasted - How America Is Losing Up to 40 Percent of Its Food from Farm to Fork to Landfill

Fact 9: Carpooling and Public Transit Savings

Fact: Carpooling or using public transit can save you up to $2,000 per year in fuel, maintenance, and parking costs.

Explanation: Sharing rides reduces the number of vehicles on the road, lowering fuel consumption, and vehicle wear and tear, and saving on parking expenses.

Reference: American Public Transportation Association: The Benefits of Public Transportation

Fact 10: Reusable Items Cut Costs

Fact: Using reusable water bottles, shopping bags, and coffee cups can save the average person up to $200 per year.

Explanation: Investing in reusable items eliminates the need for single-use products, reducing waste and saving money in the long run.

Reference: NRDC: The Problem with Plastic Bottles

These facts can be used to educate and inspire individuals to take climate action while highlighting the potential for household savings.

Climate Curiosity About Consumerism and Dietary Choices as Everyday Climate Action

Climate Curiosity About Consumerism

Fact 1: Second-Hand Shopping is a Win-Win

Fact: Buying second-hand clothes saves about 0.5 kg of CO2 emissions per item compared to buying new.

Explanation: Second-hand shopping reduces the demand for new clothing production, which requires significant energy, water, and raw materials. It also helps minimize waste by extending the life of existing garments.

Reference: ThredUp: The Environmental Benefits of Thrifting

Fact 2: Digital Subscriptions Save Trees

Fact: Switching to digital subscriptions for newspapers and magazines can save up to 1 million trees annually if adopted widely.

Explanation: Digital subscriptions reduce the need for paper production, which involves deforestation, water usage, and energy consumption. It also cuts down on waste associated with disposing of old print publications.

Reference: The World Counts: Paper Waste Facts

Fact 3: Repairing Saves Money and the Planet

Fact: Repairing electronic devices instead of replacing them can save up to 25% of the CO2 emissions compared to manufacturing new ones.

Explanation: Repairing extends the lifespan of products, reducing the demand for new resources and energy used in manufacturing. It also decreases electronic waste, which can be hazardous to the environment.

Reference: iFixit: The Repair Revolution

Fact 4: Renting Instead of Buying

Fact: Renting items like tools, party supplies, or sports equipment can reduce your carbon footprint by up to 70%.

Explanation: Renting decreases the need for producing new items, which involves raw material extraction, manufacturing processes, and transportation. It also encourages sharing and reduces waste.

Reference: Shareable: The Benefits of Renting

Fact 5: Conscious Consumerism

Fact: Consumers who choose sustainable brands can reduce their individual carbon footprint by up to 30%.

Explanation: Sustainable brands often use eco-friendly materials, ethical production processes, and minimal packaging. Supporting these brands encourages the market to adopt greener practices.

Reference: Forbes: The Rise of Conscious Consumerism

Climate Curiosity About Dietary Choices

Fact 1: Meatless Mondays Make a Difference

Fact: If everyone in the U.S. skipped meat one day a week, it would save the carbon equivalent of taking 7.6 million cars off the road.

Explanation: Meat production is resource-intensive, requiring large amounts of water, feed, and land. It also generates significant greenhouse gas emissions. Reducing meat consumption, even slightly, can lower your carbon footprint.

Reference: Meatless Monday: Environmental Benefits

Fact 2: Plant-Based Diets Are Climate-Friendly

Fact: Adopting a plant-based diet can reduce your carbon footprint by up to 50%.

Explanation: Plant-based foods generally have a lower carbon footprint compared to animal products. They require less water, land, and energy to produce and generate fewer greenhouse gas emissions.

Reference: The Lancet: The Planetary Health Diet

Fact 3: Local Foods Are Less Carbon Intensive

Fact: Eating locally grown food can reduce the carbon emissions associated with transportation by up to 90%.

Explanation: Local foods travel shorter distances from farm to plate, reducing the need for long-haul transportation, which is a significant source of carbon emissions.

Reference: NRDC: Eat Local

Fact 4: Food Waste Matters

Fact: Reducing food waste could save an average of $1,500 per year for a family of four and significantly lower methane emissions from landfills.

Explanation: Food waste contributes to methane emissions, a potent greenhouse gas. Proper planning, storing, and using leftovers can help reduce waste and save money.

Reference: NRDC: Wasted - How America Is Losing Up to 40 Percent of Its Food from Farm to Fork to Landfill

Fact 5: Seasonal Eating is Sustainable

Fact: Eating seasonal produce can reduce your food's carbon footprint by 10%.

Explanation: Seasonal produce requires fewer resources to grow and typically involves less transportation and storage time. This reduces the carbon emissions associated with off-season farming practices and long-distance shipping.

Reference: Seasonal Food Guide: Benefits of Eating Seasonal

These facts highlight how everyday choices in consumerism and diet can significantly impact climate action. Including them in a book can educate readers on the tangible benefits of sustainable living.

Climate Curiosity About Individual Action and Human Health

F act 1: Cleaner Air Improves Health

Fact: Switching to renewable energy sources can prevent up to 4.5 million premature deaths annually from air pollution.

Explanation: Fossil fuel combustion releases pollutants like particulate matter, nitrogen oxides, and sulfur dioxide, which contribute to respiratory and cardiovascular diseases. Transitioning to cleaner energy sources reduces these harmful emissions, improving air quality and public health.

Reference: World Health Organization: Ambient Air Pollution

Fact 2: Active Transportation Boosts Well-being

Fact: Walking or biking for just 30 minutes a day can reduce the risk of cardiovascular disease by up to 50%.

Explanation: Active transportation, such as walking and biking, promotes physical activity, which is crucial for cardiovascular health. It also reduces reliance on vehicles, lowering greenhouse gas emissions and improving air quality.

Reference: American Heart Association: Benefits of Physical Activity

Fact 3: Green Spaces Enhance Mental Health

Fact: Spending time in green spaces can reduce stress and improve mental health, lowering the risk of depression by up to 30%.

Explanation: Access to parks and natural environments encourages physical activity, social interaction, and relaxation, all of which are beneficial for mental health. Green spaces also help mitigate urban heat islands and improve air quality.

Reference: National Institutes of Health: Nature Contact and Human Health

Fact 4: Plant-Based Diets Lower Disease Risk

Fact: Adopting a plant-based diet can reduce the risk of developing type 2 diabetes by 23%.

Explanation: Plant-based diets are rich in fiber, antioxidants, and healthy fats, which help regulate blood sugar levels and reduce inflammation. They also lower the carbon footprint associated with food production.

Reference: Harvard T.H. Chan School of Public Health: The Nutrition Source

Fact 5: Reducing Meat Consumption Benefits Health

Fact: Reducing red and processed meat consumption can lower the risk of colorectal cancer by up to 18%.

Explanation: High consumption of red and processed meats is linked to an increased risk of colorectal cancer. Eating more plant-based foods not only reduces this risk but also benefits the environment by lowering greenhouse gas emissions from livestock.

Reference: World Health Organization: Q&A on the Carcinogenicity of the Consumption of Red Meat and Processed Meat

Fact 6: Renewable Energy Reduces Asthma Attacks

Fact: Reducing fossil fuel use and increasing renewable energy can decrease asthma attacks by 50% in children.

Explanation: Fossil fuel combustion produces pollutants that can trigger asthma attacks and other respiratory issues. Cleaner air from renewable energy sources reduces these pollutants, leading to better respiratory health.

Reference: American Lung Association: Clean Air Future

Fact 7: Efficient Homes Improve Indoor Air Quality

Fact: Homes with energy-efficient upgrades have better indoor air quality, reducing respiratory illnesses by 25%.

Explanation: Energy-efficient homes often include better ventilation systems and insulation, which help reduce indoor air pollutants such as mold, dust, and volatile organic compounds (VOCs), leading to improved respiratory health.

Reference: U.S. Department of Energy: Home Energy Efficiency and Health

Fact 8: Urban Trees Reduce Heat-Related Illnesses

Fact: Urban trees can reduce heat-related illnesses by providing shade and cooling the air, potentially lowering the risk of heatstroke by 20%.

Explanation: Trees in urban areas provide shade and release water vapor, cooling the surrounding air and reducing the urban heat island effect. This helps protect vulnerable populations, especially during heatwaves.

Reference: USDA Forest Service: Urban Forests and Human Health

Fact 9: Sustainable Agriculture Supports Nutrition

Fact: Sustainable farming practices can improve soil health, leading to more nutritious crops and reducing the risk of nutrient deficiencies.

Explanation: Sustainable agriculture practices, such as crop rotation and organic farming, enhance soil fertility and promote biodiversity. This results in healthier, more nutrient-dense food, contributing to better overall health.

Reference: FAO: Sustainable Agriculture

Fact 10: Reducing Food Waste Enhances Food Security

Fact: Cutting food waste in half could improve food security for millions and reduce malnutrition rates.

Explanation: Reducing food waste ensures that more food reaches those in need, addressing hunger and malnutrition. It also conserves resources and reduces greenhouse gas emissions from food production and waste.

Reference: FAO: Food Wastage Footprint

These facts illustrate the interconnected benefits of climate action on human health, encouraging sustainable practices that improve both environmental and personal well-being.

If you found this 2-in-1 book bundle helpful, we would appreciate it if you left a favorable review on Amazon!

www.ingramcontent.com/pod-product-compliance
Lightning Source LLC
Chambersburg PA
CBHW070121030426
42335CB00016B/2223